MODERN HUMORIST

presents

My First Presidentiary

a Scrapbook
by George W. Bush

Copyright © 2001 by Modern Humorist

Published by Three Rivers Press, New York, New York.
Member of the Crown Publishing Group.

Random House, Inc. New York, Toronto, London, Sydney, Auckland
www.randomhouse.com

THREE RIVERS PRESS is a registered trademark and the Three Rivers Press colophon is a trademark of Random House, Inc.

Printed in the United States of America

Design by Modern Humorist

Library of Congress Cataloging-in-Publication Data is available upon request.

ISBN 0-609-80818-4

10 9 8 7 6 5 4 3 2 1

First Edition

MODERN HUMORIST

presents

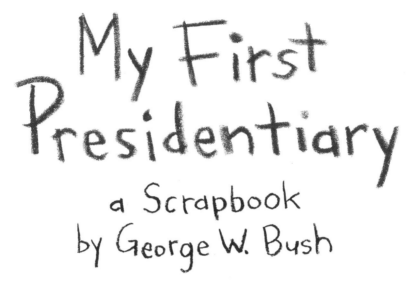

My First Presidentiary

a Scrapbook by George W. Bush

WRITTEN AND DRAWN BY
Kevin Guilfoile and John Warner

EDITED BY
Michael Colton

ADDITIONAL MATERIAL BY
John Aboud, Patrick Broderick, Martha Keavney, Daniel Radosh,
Alexandra Ringe, and Noam Weinstein

Thanks to Tommy, Haley, Jack, Joe, Will, Blair,
Erin, and Meghan for the help coloring.

SPECIAL THANKS TO
Kate Barker, Rebecca Clement, TJ Connelly, Jim Coudal,
Dave Eggers, Pete Fornatale, Louis Giliberti, Mo Guilfoile, JKHFPLA,
Eric Kissack, Dyna Moe, Nick Nadel, Sara Parikh and everyone else at LJS,
Steve Ross, Kathy Sennello and the Sennello family, Michael Sloan,
the Warner family, Kim Witherspoon, Steve Zimet,
and last but not least, Justice Antonin Scalia

MODERN HUMORIST FOUNDERS
John Aboud and Michael Colton

THREE RIVERS PRESS • NEW YORK

ABOUT THE AUTHORS

MODERN HUMORIST is a Brooklyn-based entertainment empire that produces an award-winning daily comedy magazine at www.ModernHumorist.com. Modern Humorist also produces material for *Time*, *Fortune*, *TV Guide* and National Public Radio, and is publishing its second book, a satire of popular culture, in fall 2001.

KEVIN GUILFOILE, a Modern Humorist contributing editor, is an Emmy Award–winning writer and producer of television commercials. He is a frequent contributor to *McSweeney's* and his work has also appeared in the *New Republic*.

JOHN WARNER, a Modern Humorist contributing editor, is a Hooper Award–winning short story writer and contributing editor to *McSweeney's*. He holds master's degrees in English literature and creative writing from McNeese State University, where he studied with Pulitzer Prize–winner Robert Olen Butler.

GEORGE W. BUSH, a Modern Humorist contributing editor, is the 43rd President of the United States. He lives in Washington, D.C.

For additional material, please visit
www.georgewscrapbook.com and
www.modernhumorist.com.

The Supreme Court of the United States of America

I, **George Herbert Walker Bush**
_____

Patriarch of Conservative Political Dynasty

give permission for  ~~Jebediah~~ Bush
_____

Scion of Patriarch of Conservative
Political Dynasty

to be President of the United States of America.

Date: 12/4/00   Signed: _George H. W. Bush_

☐ Check here to participate in hot lunch program (75 cents/day). Milk is provided.

Choose one of the following to participate in the "Old Conservative Hand on the Policy Steering Wheel" program:

☒ Dick Cheney   ☐ Cap Weinberger

☐ Bob Dole   ☐ ~~H.R. Haldeman~~

Dear Hector,

I'm George! Your pen pax! Condi Rice gave me your name and said we could write to each other so I could learn what other countries are like. This is important if I'm going to be president (or, as you would say "El Presidente"). I haven't traveled very much (I'm SO bad at that "Where In The ~~Hell~~ world (no bad words, please!) is Carmen San ~~Francisco~~ Diego") but I have been to your country, Meh-hes-ko. When I was in college (La Universiación Universidad), my "amigos" and I ~~me~~ used to go ~~≠~~ across the border to Metamoros where you could buy Coronas for a quarter and then pay one of the kids who sell Chic~~X~~lets $1 to carry the cases back to the border.

Me→ ←Jeb

chicklets

That's called "Free Trade" even though it costs a dollar. That's why we need to be friends with the Mexicans, because American children are too lazy to sell Chiclets in the street, or carry college kids' beer, or build Camaros.

Your "Pen" Pal, George W.

"Bitchin' Camaro"

no bad words please!!

Assignment #1

Getting to know your staff. In the space below each name, draw pictures or write words that will help you remember the names of the people who will be working for you in your administration.

Colin Powell
Secretary of State

Condoleezza Rice
National Security Advisor

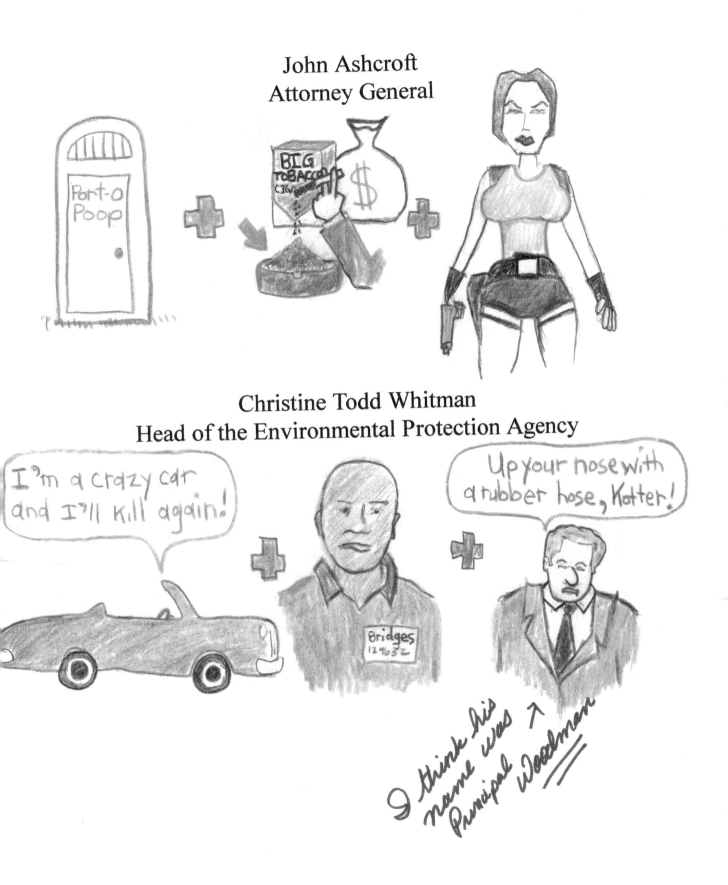

memo

To: Director, Secret Service

From: George

Please do these things:

1. ~~Steal~~ Steal Tom Daschle's toupee
2. Change my code name to "Shazam" or "Night Rider."
3. Outfit the fellas in Dick Tracy yellow raincoats
4. Give Jeb a swirly (very, very secret)
5. Put Laser Tag room on Air Force One
6. Replace Daschle's toupee with Coonskin Cap
7. Carry me when I get sleepy
8. Build me a missle-proof suit
9. Replace Daschle's Coonskin with Rangers Cap.

Assignment #2

Read Robert Coles's "Lives of Moral Leadership," and then write a 100 word essay on how the ideas expressed in the book will affect your tenure as President.

"Lives of Moral Leadership" is a very, very, ~~very, very, very, very, very,~~ *thinks of more words* very, good book. The dictionary says a moral is "a practical lesson contained in a story." The author thinks that a good leader is a person who likes to tell stories. I like to tell stories. Sometimes my stories are about how an Irishman, an Italian and a Polish person get themselves into silly trouble. Sometimes there's also a German guy.

This is not 100 words! ✓−

Fun Things to do at Camp David:

Monday
AM: Climb on Rocks

PM: Pick up litter
around Beaver Pond

← S'more

Tuesday
AM: ~~Swim~~ Canoeing

PM: Make Windsocks

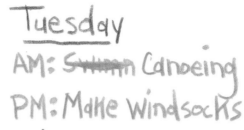

Wednesday
AM: Negotiate peace
between Palestinians
and Israelis.

PM: Ceramics

To: Yassar   From: Ehud

Thursday
AM: Meet with House
and Senate Leaders

PM: Animal Masks

Dick Gephardt   Denny Hastert

memo

To: Uncle Dick

From: George

I found these in one of Daddy's drawers. We won't even need to re-type them!

CHENEY, RICHARD
Secretary of Defense - Ext. 66
Vice President Ext. 2

BAKER, JAMES A.
Secretary of State - Ext. 54
Consiglieri - use the "special" line only in electoral emergencies

POWELL, GEN. COLIN
Chairman Joint Chiefs - Ext. 375
Secretary of States Ext. 54

RUMSFELD, DONALD

Dir. Office of Economic Opportunity
Ext. 154

Pres. Ford Chief of Staff - Ext. 20

Secretary of Defense - Ext. 66

Secretary of Defense Ext. 66

VENEMAN, ANN

Dept. Sec. Dept. of Agriculture
Ext. 4865

Secretary of Agriculture

Secretary of Agriculture Ext. 4800

CHAVEZ, LINDA

Director Civil Rights Comission
Ext. 7652

Secretary of Labor

Ext. 70

Dear Hector,

Sorry I haven't written in so long. I thought having a "home office" would mean I'd get to sleep in and stuff but I'm working more hours than ever! I've been missing a lot of my T.V. programs too. The only time I get to see Law and Order anymore is when A and E shows a rerun late at night, but lots of times that will be a George Dzundza or a Paul Sorvino instead of

Paul
Sorvino
→

← Jerry
Orbach

a Jerry Orbach. Jerry Orbach is my favorite actor. He was the dad in "Dirty Dancing". Do you get "Dirty Dancing" in Mexico, or do the video stores only get the Salma Hayek ← Hubba Hubba! movies?

"~~Nobody~~ ~~No one~~ puts Baby in a corner!"
— Patrick Swayze in Dirty Dancing

Baby →

I think Jerry Orbach would make a better president then Martin Sheen.

Your pal,

George

Assignment #3
The defense budget is roughly $280 billion.
How would you allocate these funds?

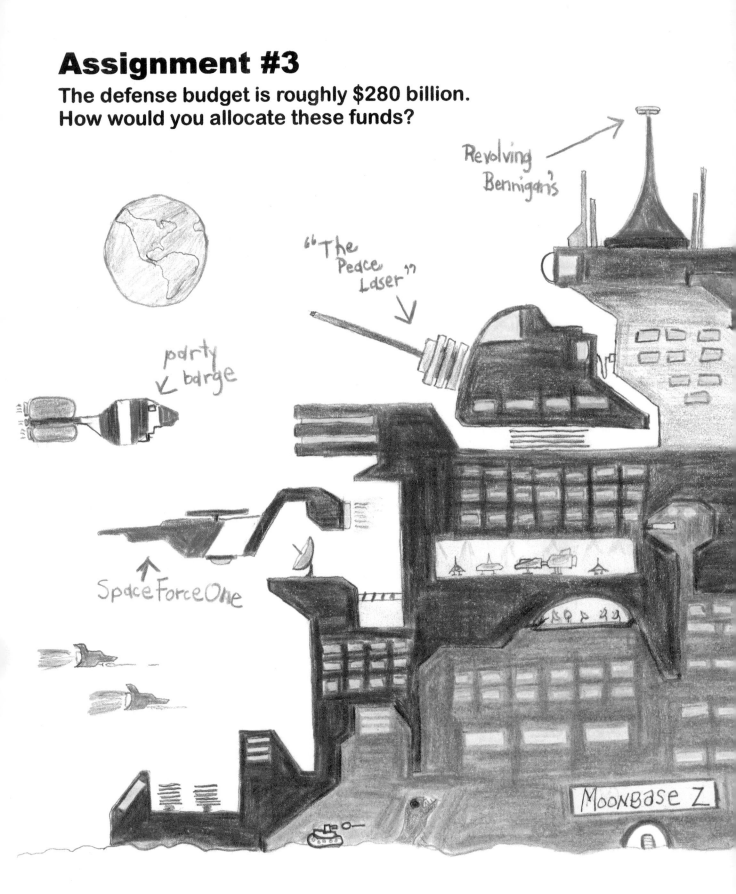

To: White House waitresses

From: George

In future State dinners, please make sure I get the Aquaman glass. It looks very bad if I get the glass with the bad guy on it and the leader of another country gets the glass with the good guy on it. Here's a drawing that might help you remember.

To: Andy Card

From: George

Uncle Dick gave me a really good book about the Presidents and it got me thinking about my legacy. All the great Presidents had a cool nickname like "F. D. R.," and "Old Tippy Canoe," and "Daddy." I should have a cool nickname too. On the attached page are some nicknames that I think would be good for me, but ask around and see if anybody's got any other ideas.

Nicknames for me:

1. Dubya Dutch

2. P.B.J.

3. The Father of His Children

4. Chico

5. The Man

6. The Dub-Dub-Dub-Dub-Dubya-Bee

7. Squinty McGinty

8. (George) Walker (Bush former owner of the) Texas Ranger (s)

9. The Funky Phantom

10. The Great Pronounciator

11. The American Ronald Reagan

To: George

From: George

Notes on handling the media:

Do's

1. Kiss the evenhanded and straight-shooting Bill O'Reilly's ring.

2. Tell that MTV News fox Tabitha Soren that I wear mine "very brief."

3. Send gift basket to Cousin John thanking him for his objectivity on election night.

4. Always have Uncle Dick explain when Maureen Dowd is making fun of me.

5. Tell Katie Couric what a difference Today makes.

Do not's

1. Go on that Tim Russet's show. Too many questions.

2. Look ~~once~~ directly into Helen Thomas's gaze.

3. Have a press conference.

4. Let self be blinded by glare from Sam Donaldson's forehead.

5. Let Jann Wenner airbrush the package.

Dear Hector,

There are basically three types of medals I get to give out. The easiest way to get one is to be a Prisoner of War. That one is pretty much automatic. Another way is to be a famous singer who uses her ~~famousness~~ celebrity to go on Larry King and tell all of her crazy fans how to vote. Most of Bill Clinton's medals were this kind.

ABSOLUTELY MY FINAL SHOW FOR THE LAST TIME SPECIAL

The other medal I can give is The President's Award For Physical Fitness, but it's really hard to get. You have to do like a jillion sit-ups. That's why I've invented a new medal: The Vice President's Award For Physical Fitness. To get it, you only need to do more sit-ups than Uncle Dick.

Your pal,
George

Assignment #4

good penmanship

Handwriting and conservative values. Copy the following quotes by Senator Trent Lott in cursive (no printing!).

"The spirit of [Confederate President] Jefferson Davis lives in the 1984 Republican platform." *To the Sons of Confederate Veterans in Biloxi, Mississippi.*

The spirit of [Confederate President] Jefferson Davis lives in the 1984 Republican platform.

"Are coeds afraid to walk across the college campus at night? Perhaps we should authorize ROTC units to teach marksmanship even to the students who are not enrolled in a military program." *From his keynote address at the NRA's 127th convention.*

Are coeds afraid to walk across the college campus at night? Perhaps we should authorize R.O.T.C. units to teach marksmanship even to the students who are not enrolled in a military program.

"You should try to show [homosexuals] a way to deal with that problem, just like alcoholism or sex addiction or kleptomania." *On Armstrong Williams's radio show,* The Right Side, *June 15, 1998.*

You should try to show [homosexuals] a way to deal with that problem, just like alcoholism or sex addiction or kleptomania.

Proposed White House Renovations

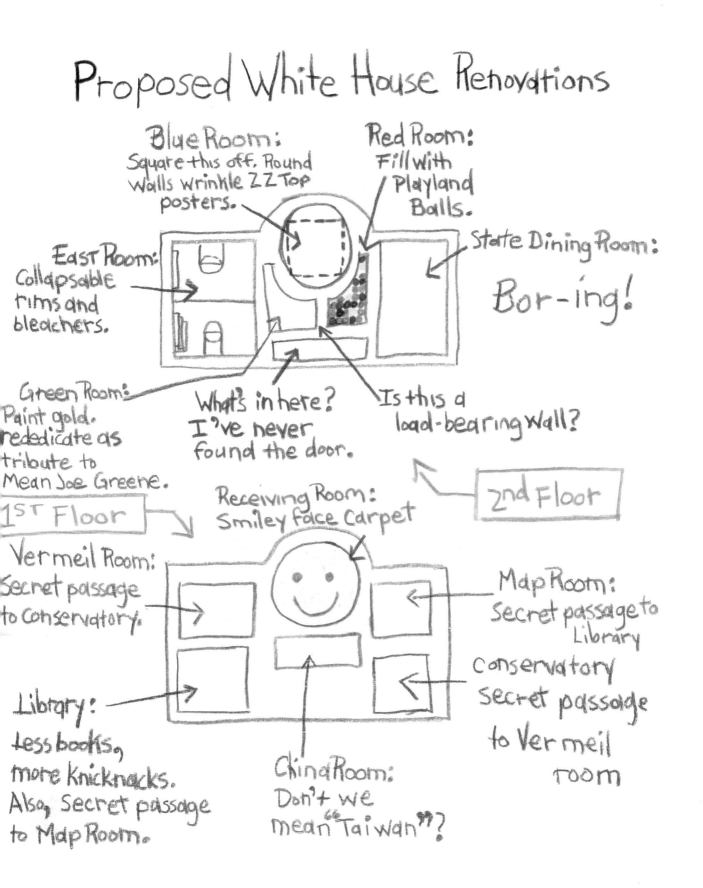

Blue Room: Square this off. Round walls wrinkle ZZ Top posters.

Red Room: Fill with Playland Balls.

State Dining Room: Bor-ing!

East Room: Collapsable rims and bleachers.

Green Room: Paint gold. rededicate as tribute to Mean Joe Greene.

What's in here? I've never found the door.

Is this a load-bearing wall?

1ST Floor

2nd Floor

Receiving Room: Smiley face Carpet

Vermeil Room: Secret passage to Conservatory.

Map Room: Secret passage to Library

Library: Less books, more knicknacks. Also, Secret passage to Map Room.

conservatory Secret passage to Vermeil room

China Room: Don't we mean "Taiwan"?

To: Treasury Secretary Paul O'Neill memo
From: George

   Just in case somebody decides they want
to change the money again, here's one idea.
It's up to you guys of course, but
if anybody needs a picture of me and
Daddy to do this, I have a good
one that Mommy took on our boat.

	George	Jeb (the butthead)
1955 Crazy Eights	25	1
1959 tock/paper/scissors	8	65
1960 "Who-Loves-Mom-more" hugging Contest	1	0
1962-2000 RISK	0	356
1965 Tic Tac Toe	465 ties	
1974 Beeropoly	48	6
1977 Pong	934	0
1972, 76, 80 Beer Bong Olympics	4	0
1990's Governor of major state	1 I was first!	1
1996 Crash Bandicoot	50	0
1997 Crash Bandicoot 2	345	0
2000 President	I kicked his ass!	

Assignment #5
Asian studies and creative writing.

Haiku is a form of Japanese poetry. It does not rhyme. Each haiku has three lines. The first line has five syllables. The second line has seven syllables. The third line has five syllables.

Here is an example of haiku from the master Basho:

> In my life's autumn
> Dying, at last I wonder
> How goes my neighbor?

In the space below, take a moment to express your deepest emotions by using the haiku form. *Are you sure this is your deepest emotia*

Very good movie

Mr. Holland's Opus makes

Me cry at the end.

Look what I found on Karl Rove's desk!

memo

CONFIDENTIAL

this was a good E.R.!

Date: February 1, 2000
To: White House Staff
CC: James Baker
Subject: Emergency procedures for the "Vice" President in case of (cardiac episode)

IN CASE OF A HEART ATTACK BY "VICE" PRESIDENT CHENEY

1. Do not panic.

2. Check "Vice" Presidential pulse. Perform resuscitative measures as necessary. Rush to hospital.

3. Regardless of condition, inform media that "Vice" President is "resting comfortably and looking forward to getting back to doing the work of the American people."

4. Have Secret Service suggest a nap for the President.

5. When President awakes from nap, suggest a nice game of "Operation" or "Life." ← *You're married! Receive tax penalty!*

6. If President asks for whereabouts of "Vice" President, say, "I just saw him heading towards the [location which cannot be verified]." Repeat as necessary.

7. If condition of "Vice" President remains unknown, remind President of how "freaky," "cool" and "underrated" the Alan Parker-directed film version of *Pink Floyd The Wall* is, and ask if he wouldn't like to see it again in the special White House "black light" room. *"Teacher! Leave no kids behind!"*

8. In case of "Vice" Presidential demise, tell President that Uncle Dick is now living on a farm in the country with other ex-Vice Presidents and retired oil executives.

9. Call James Baker on his crypt phone. Panic.

memo

To: Secretary of Education Rod Paige

From: George

Rod,

Can we print some of these up
for the poor kids?

To: Andy Card

From: George

I just found out that every President who was elected in a year with a zero has either been shot or died in office, And 2000 ends in three zeroes!

Below, I've worked up some disguises to protect me whenever I go out in public.

Data from Star Trek TNG

A Lion

Dancing Banana

Jeb

Dear Hector,

Who is your favorite super hero?
Laura says I look just like Dr. Reed
Richards of the Fantastic Four. If
I were Reed Richards I would solve
all of the world's problems with
my special brand of ~~magic stretchy~~
~~powers.~~ compassionate conservatism.

Sorry fellas.
Not too close!

←Me
(Mr.
Fantastic!)

← The conservative
ultra right wing
Republicans

The Fantastic Four got their powers when their spaceship was bombarded by gamma rays. Even though the Fantastic Four are the coolest, I'm going to ask Congress to investigate where these gamma rays are coming from because some people, like Saddam Hussein ~~people the~~ or Magneto, might use their Fantastic powers for evil instead of good.

Saddam Hu-thing →
(Not a tracing!)
very good!

I must have Kuwait!

your pal,
George

Assignment #6

World Leaders Word Search. This assignment has two parts. First, fill in the missing section of each world leader's name. Then, find and circle the name in the word search. The names can be horizontal or vertical, forward or backward, but not diagonal.

Angola
President Jose Eduardo _RYPYGIDY_

Azerbaijan
President Heydar _BHQ NGFZ_

Djibouti
President _PXLIGGG_
Ismail Omar

Estonia
President Lennart _ZWSWTSM_

Equatorial Guinea
President Brig. Gen. (Ret.)
Teodoro _OBIANG NGUEMA MBASOGO_

Kyrgyzstan
President Askar _KHJMXYLCTY_

Laos
President _EUEBSXN_
Siphandon

Oman
Sultan and Prime Minister _BLTLUQXZY_ bin Said Al Said

Paraguay
President Luis _OPRQGG_ Macchi

Yemen
President Lt. Gen. Ali Abdallah _EJXAGD_

Venezuela
President Hugo _BOSS_ Frias

a hard one!

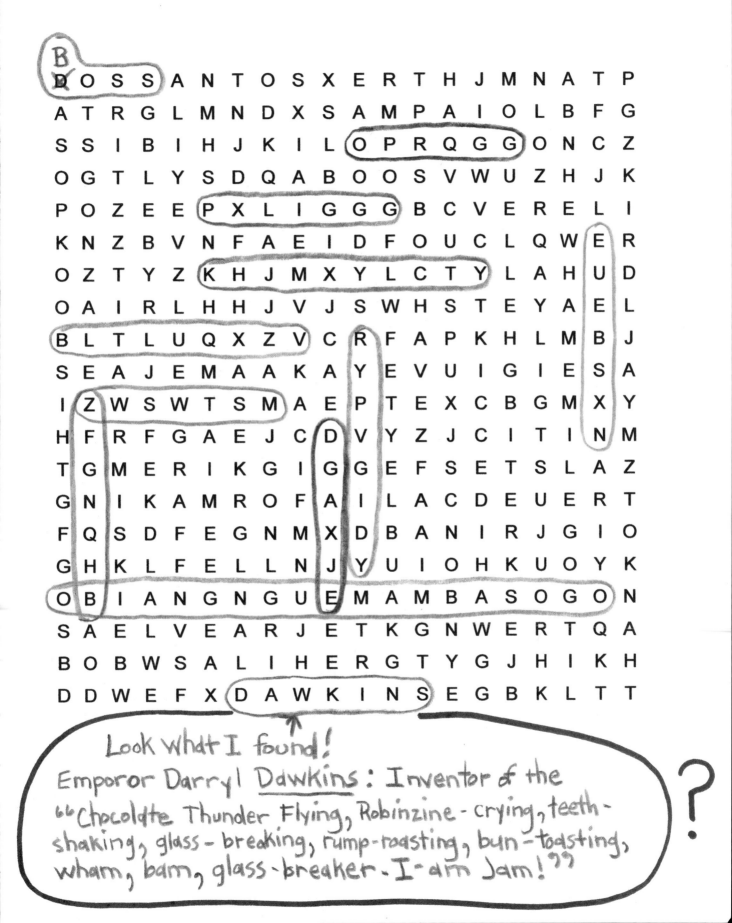

B
D O S S A N T O S X E R T H J M N A T P
A T R G L M N D X S A M P A I O L B F G
S S I B I H J K I L O P R Q G G O N C Z
O G T L Y S D Q A B O O S V W U Z H J K
P O Z E E P X L I G G G B C V E R E L I
K N Z B V N F A E I D F O U C L Q W E R
O Z T Y Z K H J M X Y L C T Y L A H U D
O A I R L H H J V J S W H S T E Y A E L
B L T L U Q X Z V C R F A P K H L M B J
S E A J E M A A K A Y E V U I G I E S A
I Z W S W T S M A E P T E X C B G M X Y
H F R F G A E J C D V Y Z J C I T I N M
T G M E R I K G I G G E F S E T S L A Z
G N I K A M R O F A I L A C D E U E R T
F Q S D F E G N M X D B A N I R J G I O
G H K L F E L L N J Y U I O H K U O Y K
O B I A N G N U E M A M B A S O G O N
S A E L V E A R J E T K G N W E R T Q A
B O B W S A L I H E R G T Y G J H I K H
D D W E F X D A W K I N S E G B K L T T

Look what I found!
Emporor Darryl Dawkins: Inventor of the
"Chocolate Thunder Flying, Robinzine - crying, teeth-
shaking, glass - breaking, rump-roasting, bun-toasting,
wham, bam, glass-breaker. I-am Jam!"

?

The White House
Washington, D.C.

Dear Mumia Abu-Jamal,

Thank you so much for your recent request for clemency. Unfortunately, I have to deny the request and reccommend that plans go ahead for your execution.

It makes me very sad that you, the N.B.A.'s all-time leading scorer, have gotten yourself in so much trouble. Why couldn't you have turned out more like Michael Jordan, who is part-owner of a terrible basketball team? Or how about Wilt

"The Stilt" Chamberlain, who wrote a sexy autobiography? I haven't read every little detail of your case, but spoiled professional athletes like you have to be taught a lesson that they can't go around demanding outrageous salaries and shooting cops and other authority figures.

Your pal,

George

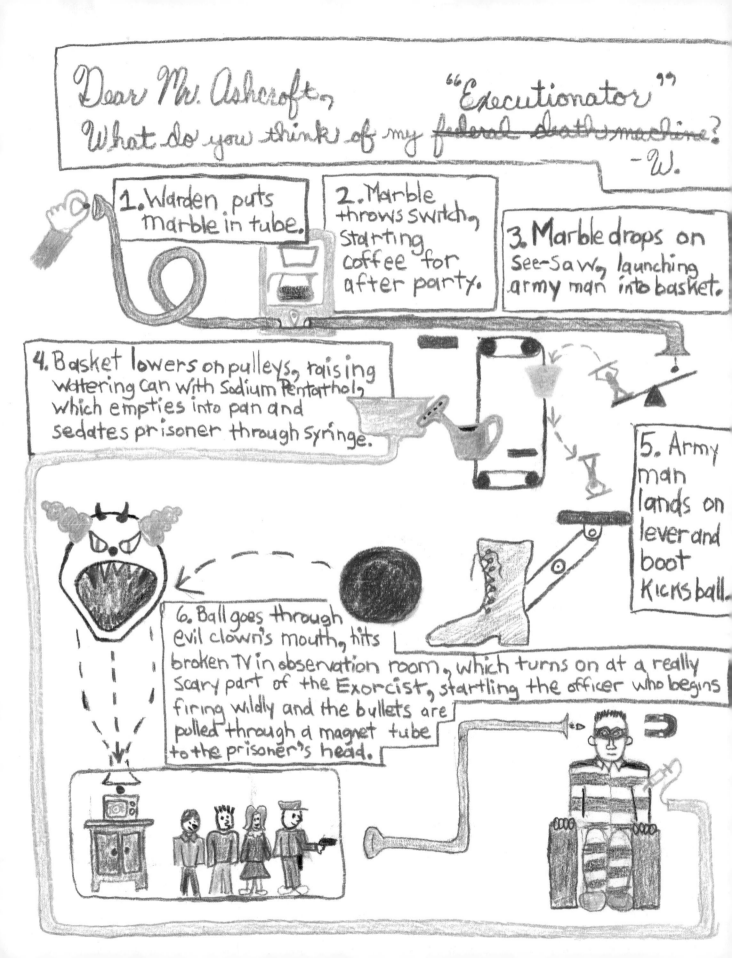

Assignment #7

Leave No Child Behind Maze. Sally, Cletus, and Marcus have all been failed by the Clinton Administration's inability to stand up to the teachers' union in order to establish fair and objective criteria by which students and their teachers are measured.

Since you have pledged to leave no child behind, you must help Sally, Cletus, and Marcus through the maze of bureaucratic red tape and organized labor to the land of educational opportunity and the promise of a better future for all of America's children.

These directions are long! I had Karl tell me what they said!

Sally

Marcus

Cletus

mr. Gorbachey, Tear down this wall!

see me!

Can I go through this little hole? How big am I?

1. 2. 3.

too big!

He can go through!

oops!

Dear Mr. Castro,

How are you? I'm fine. You should let your people have more freedom. Maybe you should give them all guns. Just a thought.

Anyway, you've probably heard about our baseball problems. The strike zone is too small and all the batters are juiced up on steroids til they're bigger than Bruce Banner stuck in ▓ rush-hour traffic.

We need pitching. And you've got it. So I'm willing to trade you the Florida Keys

Grrr! Lengthy Delays make Hulk mad!

HYUNDAI

for five left-handed starters and some boat people to be named later (My brother Jeb is the Governor of Florida and he's not getting re-elected anyway. Long story.)

Say, how's the arm on that Elian kid? In 15 years or so, he could be bigger than Slammin' Sammy Sosa (is Sosa one of yours too? I can't keep all those islands straight).

We've got some other stuff you might want too, like Gloria Estefan tapes (We've all got CD players up here so nobody wants them).

Okay. Let me know.

Your pal,
George

memo

To: Jeb

From: George

I feel bad about the election stuff in Florida. Mr. Delay says that Democrats designed the welfare system, so it's no wonder that the ballots they designed don't work either (that got a big laugh at the club).

That's why I invented this new voting machine. Everybody loves bowling! Election Day could be like a big birthday party! Wouldn't it have been neat if I got to be president on election night and I also got a Game Boy?

"The Vote-inerator"

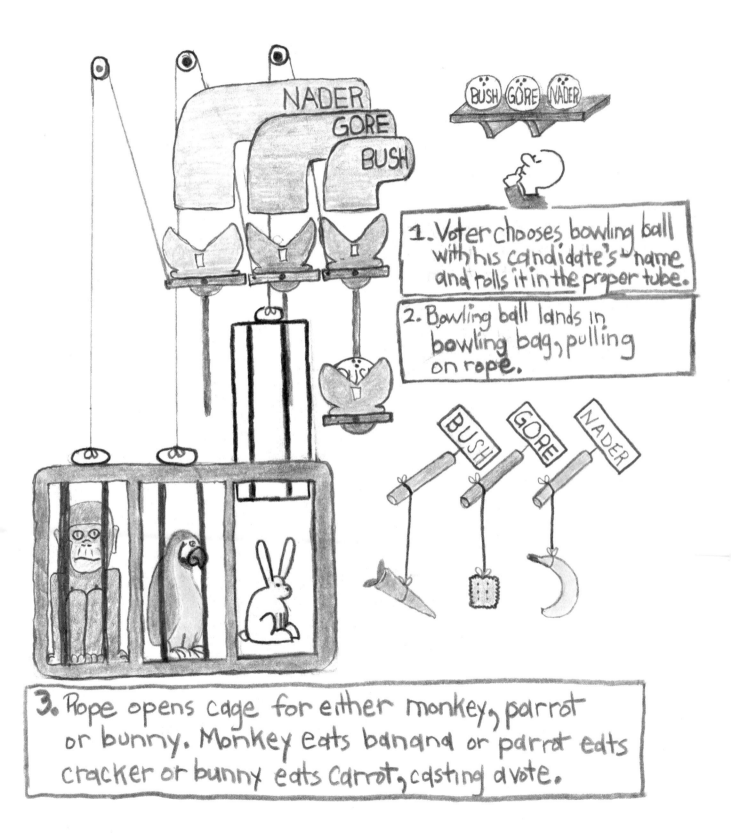

Assignment #8

Tax Cut Compromise. Imagine that obstructionist Democrats in Congress, bent on placing political gain over the well-being of American families, filibuster over your fair, equitable, and easy-to-calculate, across-the-board tax cut.

For each of the following examples, write a brief, sound-bite-length answer that outlines the amount of damage the Democrats have wrought in their failure to provide tax relief to these families, with their short-sightedness and pointless posturing. Make sure to consider all the information provided when formulating your answer.

1. Robert Walters and his wife, Susan Smythe-Walters, make $1,845,326 a year in stock dividends on investments originally made by Susan Smythe-Walters's grandfather. They earn an additional $2,456,325 each year from Robert's largely ceremonial position as president of a manufacturing company (originally founded by Susan Smythe-Walters's grandfather) that keeps our nation humming by employing many workers in minimum-wage jobs. Robert and Susan have no children because they believe that children are "messy" and "inconvenient," especially when it comes to jetting off for long weekends in Switzerland, and therefore they feel that strangers' children should not benefit from their wealth (and rightfully so), and besides, wouldn't those people looking for government handouts be better off following the example of Susan Smythe-Walters's grandfather, who pulled himself up by his bootstraps as a teenager by selling plums on the street during the Depression, thus starting the empire that would ensure that his heirs could live comfortably in perpetuity? Robert and Susan's accountant is named Milt, and last year the Walterses purchased him a new-model Buick LeSabre in gratitude for "his fine, fine work" (wink-wink, nudge-nudge).

Smythe INTERNATIONAL Plum-Making Corp.

It's a sad day when money earned cannot be spent likewise.

good!

2. "George Doe" and his wife, Laura, make $432,000 in interest each year on money George extracted from a failed oil venture prior to its dissolution, and an additional $654,000 that George earns as a figurehead president of an American League baseball team, purchased largely with other people's money.

George's father is president of a large North American country.

George and Laura have twin daughters who call the Does' accountant "Uncle Milt."

How could anyone be afraid of or against "affirmative advancement?"

Yes! They will never figure out what that means

3. Tim Robbins and Susan Sarandon are a Hollywood "power couple." Susan is considered an "A" list acting talent and currently receives between $5 million and $7 million per movie. Tim receives less money per movie than Susan, but is also less choosy about his roles and, for additional income, directs one film encompassing a borderline socialist message every three years or so.

Susan is older than Tim, but remains appealing in an "aging yet still confident and sexy" way.

Tim and Susan give copious amounts of time and money to left-wing extremist causes that threaten the moral fabric of our nation.

Despite being unmarried, Tim and Susan have chosen to have many, many children together, one of whom is named Milt.

With my tax cut maybe correct *they can finally have enough money so they can stop whining and go back to making GOOD movies like "Bull Durham."*

memo

Date: March 3, 2000
To: White House Staff
CC: James Baker
Subject: Emergency procedures in case the "Vice" President has an attack of conscience over the Bush administration's ties to big oil.

IN CASE OF AN ATTACK OF CONSCIENCE BY "VICE" PRESIDENT CHENEY

1. Do not panic.

2. Explain again to the "Vice" President the important role our nation's oil producers play in our economy and our national security.

3. Next, remind "Vice" President of how grateful the nation's oil producers are to the Bush administration and its willingness to foster a "responsible" drilling policy that doesn't kowtow to the dangerous and extreme environmental nutcases and that this gratitude will be repaid with very generous support for the 2004 campaign.

4. As last measure, leak interior documents of sweetheart deals "Vice" President oversaw as secretary of defense that benefitted subsidiary of company that would come to pay him millions of dollars in salary and stock options upon his leaving government.

5. Panic. Then call James Baker.

I found this one in the trash looking for some gum I threw out by accident.

Miami Vice President

Cover me, Tubbs!

Assignment #9

Solve the puzzle that identifies some of the different threats to your administration.

(aka "Darth Sidious")

Across

1. Senator Hillary *Palpatine*
2. Congressman Richard *Kimball*
3. General *Malomar* Gadaffi
4. Sustained economic *Freshness*
5. ABC News anchor Peter *Brady*
6. Former President Bill *Rosavelt*

Down

7. Osama Bin *ARKIN*
8. Senator Tom *ARNOLD*
9. Senator *LEM* Daschle
10. The New York *GROOVE*
11. Leader of Parliament Funkadelic George *DUBYA!*

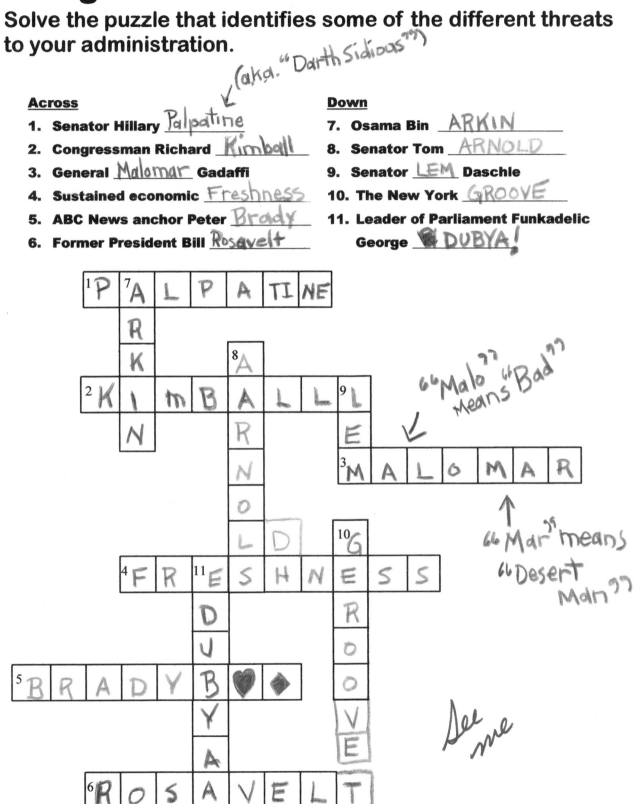

"Malo" means "Bad"

"Mar" means "Desert Man"

See me

Dear Hector,

Thanks for your letter. Wow! I didn't know a person could walk so many miles to school without shoes. Maybe if we moved a shoe factory to your town you could work there and they could pay you in shoes for making shoes.

George!
(blah, blah, Something) political Viability! (blah, Something

←Laura

There was a time when my life was really tough. I'd just ~~gotten bucked by Laura after a night I don't remember,~~ realized I had to make my family a priority and promised to ~~drink only at weddings or when it's really hot out or when it might taste good to have at tall cold one~~ never drink alcohol again.

I knew I had ~~to be smarter~~ about it ~~because Daddy was threatening to stop helping me with things, like not going to Viet Nam.~~ to do the right thing for myself and my family.

    ~~Once or twice~~ I almost ~~got busted~~ failed in my pledge. ~~again.~~ There's this videotape of me at a wedding when I was ~~stuffoced~~ in high spirits, but ~~I managed to get out of it~~ continued to find strength and keep my pledge.

    So ~~xxxxx~~ chin up my ~~little brown~~ friend. Life can turn around for you too if you ~~have wealthy and politically connected parents~~. trust in God's message and follow his guidance as you navigate the pitfalls of life.

Bienvenidos ~~Bee "N" Vaneedoes,~~

Whore-Hay (George)

Lets discuss
Maybe we shouldn't send this one!

Assignment #10

How a Bill Becomes a Law: Reading Comprehension and Vocabulary. In order to accomplish our ambitious legislative goal of refocusing government on the people's business, and therefore ending the divisive partisan bickering that has gridlocked Washington for so long, it is important that you understand the steps it takes to turn your bold new initiatives into an actual law of the land. Read the following narrative on "How a Bill Becomes a Law" and write sentences using words from the reading.

There are many stages a bill must go through before it lands on the President's desk and is signed into law.

First, there are the "good" lobbyists. The "good" lobbyists are our nation's watchdogs, always on the lookout for <u>inequities</u>, such as when gun control <u>extremists</u> try to deny the right of law-abiding Americans to use automatic weapons for sport hunting. When the "good" lobbyists identify this sort of potential harm, they alert <u>Charlton Heston</u>, who in turn alerts a sympathetic member of Congress to this potential danger to our freedoms.

Next, legislation protecting the right of Americans to own guns that shoot upward of 15 rounds per second is introduced by the congressperson. The congressperson who introduces the bill is called the bill's <u>sponsor</u>.

Once the bill is in Congress, it goes to committee, where hearings are held to discuss the bill. This is where bills frequently <u>languish</u> due to the efforts of the "bad" lobbyists. "Bad" lobbyists use money to influence liberal congresspeople to abandon their principles in favor of personal gain and filling their campaign war chests. The liberals who have been purchased by the "bad" lobbyists undermine the intent of the originally proposed law by adding amendments.

Once the bill leaves committee, it is debated by the entire congressional body and amended even further, now making the bill almost impossible to recognize when compared to its original <u>incarnation</u>. After debate is closed, the bill comes up for a vote by the entire legislative body. If the bill passes both the House of Representatives and the Senate, the bill next goes to you (the President!), where you then decide whether or not to sign or veto the bill.

If the liberal legislators go overboard with their <u>unconscionable</u> amendments, you veto the bill. If the bill furthers your agenda of bringing Americans together, you sign it, it becomes a law, and afterward you give everyone pens!

Inequities

Mr. Greenspan says that tax differed ✗
inequities are a good investment.

Extremists

Gun control extremists. ✗ *not a sentence*

Charlton Heston

Charlton Heston was really good at driving ✗
the chariot in Ben Hur.

Sponsor

If you feel like you need a drink, ✗
you should call your sponsor to talk.

Languish

English should be the official languish
of the United States. ✗

Incarnation

Chili con incarnation is a good ✗
meal for a cold day.

Unconscionable

When people drink too much,
sometimes they go unconscionable. ✗
Did you read the assignment?

<u>memo</u>

To: ~~Gail~~ Gale Norton, Secretary of the Interior

From: George

Dear Gale,

First, I want to say that I know how you gals hate the word "secretary" so feel free to put "administrative assistant of the Interior" on your business cards.

On the radio, I heard a man call you "James Watt in a skirt," which reminded Daddy of a funny story about the White House Christmas party in 1982. Ask Uncle Dick to tell it to you sometime.

I have a couple of suggestions for your department. Here are some things I do <u>not</u> want you to put on the Endangered Species list:

1. Hamburgers

2. Veal

3. Tater Tots

Broccolli and canned peas are okay to put on, though.

Also, have you seen the ~~movie~~ movie "Fire Down Below" where Steven Seagull plays an E.P.A. agent? I think all E.P.A. employees should learn Kung Fu. In the movie it really came in handy.

Your pal,
George

Assignment #11

Supreme Court: Logic and Reasoning. After reading the following statements, answer the questions using the information provided. This is a timed exercise, and you may use diagrams to help in answering.

1. Nine Supreme Court justices go to a baseball game.

2. Justices Rehnquist, Scalia, and Thomas always sit in the right-field bleachers.

3. Hot dogs cost $3.50 each, hot pretzels are $1.75 apiece, beer is $4.25, and ice cream is $2.50.

4. Justices Ginsburg, Stevens, Breyer, and Souter always sit in the extreme left-field bleachers.

5. Justice Kennedy always sits in center field.

6. Justice Breyer is lactose-intolerant.

7. Justice Stevens is a thorn in Justice Rehnquist's side.

8. Justice O'Connor usually sits in right field, except when the life of the mother is at stake, in which case she sits in left field.

9. Justice Rehnquist does his level best in steering the court to correct the outrageous actions of the liberal, activist Warren court.

10. Justice Thomas always sits on Justice Scalia's lap.

11. Anyone sitting in right field thinks (properly) that using the designated hitter only in the American League is a violation of equal protection statutes.

12. Justice Thomas does not cheer.

Questions:

1. How many tickets do the justices need in order for each justice to have a seat?

Nine, but at the Ballpark in Arlington only four have to pay.

2. In a typical display of judicial overreach, Justice Stevens buys a beer, a pretzel, a hot dog, and an ice cream for each of the justices in his section of the bleachers who wants them. How much will this cost Justice Stevens?

Nothing. Justices Scalia and Breyer will pay if Justice Stevens puts a hair on Justice Thomas's Coke.

3. If the game starts with a prayer asking Our Lord that he grant the athletes the strength and courage to perform up to their abilities and leave the field free from harm or injury, how many justices are frowning in a display of self-righteousness that denies the fact that our nation was founded on Christian principles?

Only Justices O'Connor and Ginsburg, so long as the prayer is given, not by a school official but a really hot cheerleader in a tight sweater.

4. How many beers will it take for Justice Souter to start calling Justice Ginsburg "Ruthie baby"?

Two "Thirsty-two" ouncers.

Assignment #12 *needs work*

Clinton Math Word Problems. Each of the following has only one answer. Show your work.

1. Trent Lott said that "this Hillary" has to remember that she's only one of 100 United States senators. There are 50 states. How many senators does each state have?

   This many

2. If Bill Clinton denies one-third of an inappropriate relationship with a female staffer for every year that he's President, how many inappropriate relationships with females could Bill Clinton deny over two presidential terms?

   $$\frac{(I\ did\ not\ have\ sexual\ relations\ with\ that\ woman)}{3} \times 8$$

3. If Hillary Clinton invested an initial $5,000 in pork belly futures and one year later sold them for $75,000, how much profit did she make for each month that she owned the futures? (Hint: There are 12 months in a year.)

   In the future, America's favorite sport will be hover car polo. →

4. When the country is finally rid of Bill Clinton, he will collect $100,000 per speaking engagement. Assume also that your sensible tax cut passes and he will save 10 percent of his income, which, under a Gore administration, would have been swallowed up by the out-of-control government bureaucracy. If Bill Clinton makes 10 speeches in the first year, how much money will he save?

memo

To: Andy Card

From: George

Pillowcase with Space-Age, Astronaut-tested, drool-resistant fabric

Speaker plays Posh Spice reading Harry Potter

zzzzz

Nuclear Button for first-strike capability after 10pm.

Licking patch, always tastes like Big-League Chew.

Pickup and drop-off pocket for Tooth Fairy.

Decorative

memo

To: Karl Rove

From: George

   I was in the video store today renting Mission: Impossible and it said on the box: "Expect the Impossible." What a cool campaign slogan! I spent three hours walking around the store writing down campaign slogans off the movie boxes:

Beyond the horizon lies the secret to a new beginning. -Bush/Cheney 2004 (Waterworld was cool!)

Truth needs a soldier. -Bush/Cheney 2004 (Clear and present Danger: Awesome)

The fate of a nation rests on the courage of one man. -Bush/Cheney 2004 (Air Force one: Wicked excellent!)

The sands will rise. The heavens will part. The power will be unleashed. (oh yeah—The Mummy!)
                    -Bush/Cheney 2004

The White House
Washington, D.C.

Very good, George!

Dear Hector,

Thanks for teaching me about your culture. I had lost interest in Mexico around the time I stopped drinking Tequila, but you taught me that it is an exciting country with its own music, history and two channels on my cable.

If you ever make it across the border in a ~~Rotary exchange program~~ ~~truckload of fruit~~, we could have a sleepover in the Lincoln Bedroom and we could build forts and whip those little Lincoln Logs at each other. It will be fun.

Hola for now ("hola" means both "hello" and "goodbye"!)

Your pal,

George